# Extreme

# DINOSAURS

written by
**Robert Mash**

illustrated by
**Stuart Martin**

EXCLUSIVE EDITION
SCHOLASTIC
FOR SCHOLASTIC
BOOK CLUBS
AND FAIRS

# Meet the DINOSAURS

Among the most incredible creatures ever to walk the Earth, the dinosaurs ruled our world for more than 160 million years, from the end of the Triassic period to the end of the Cretaceous period, 65 million years ago.

## The Dinosaur Dynasty

At the beginning of the Triassic period, about 250 million years ago, there were two main groups of land reptiles: the synapsids (the most numerous) and the archosaurs. However, by the end of the Triassic, about 213 million years ago, the archosaurs had taken over. These reptiles included the crocodiles, the pterosaurs and the dinosaurs. Compared with the synapsids, the dinosaurs were extreme in almost every way: bigger, fiercer and faster!

By the beginning of the Jurassic period they had seen off nearly all the land opposition. Our own ancestors, the mammals, were not much bigger than guinea pigs and hid in their burrows during the daytime, only daring to go out at night. The only other large animals were the marine reptiles, such as the plesiosaurs, and the pterosaurs, who ruled the skies.

## Examining the Evidence

Dead dinosaurs usually rotted away or were eaten. Tough parts like bones, teeth and claws sometimes hardened to stone and have been preserved as fossils. Bones tell us about the size and shape of an animal, and how the muscles were attached to them. Teeth and claws give us clues as to what the animals ate; sometimes the contents of the stomach, droppings and nests are also fossilized. Tracks of their footprints and even the impressions of a dinosaur's skin may be left. By piecing all these clues together, paleontologists can often show what the dinosaur looked like, what it ate and how it lived.

## Skin Deep

We can't know what colours dinosaurs were, but by looking at animals today we can make good guesses. Dinosaurs would have been coloured either for camouflage or with striking patterns to attract mates or intimidate rivals. Their skins were usually leathery, with bumps or knobs. Some of the smaller Cretaceous species may have had structures like feathers, which may have been brightly coloured, like many birds are today.

## The Age of Dinosaurs

| Conifers, ginkgos and seed ferns are common. Reptiles and amphibians are widespread. The first dinosaurs, crocodiles and pterosaurs appear. The first mammals appear. | Cycads, conifers and ferns flourish. The first birds appear. DINOSAURS RULE! Marine reptiles and pterosaurs take many forms. | The first flowering plants appear. Conifers flourish; cycads and ginkgos are less common. Dinosaurs remain the dominant land animals but die out at the end of the Cretaceous. Small mammals become widespread. |
| --- | --- | --- |
| **TRIASSIC** | **JURASSIC** | **CRETACEOUS** |

← **MESOZOIC PERIOD: 250–65 MILLION YEARS AGO** →

**250** million years ago     **203** mya     **135** mya     **65** mya

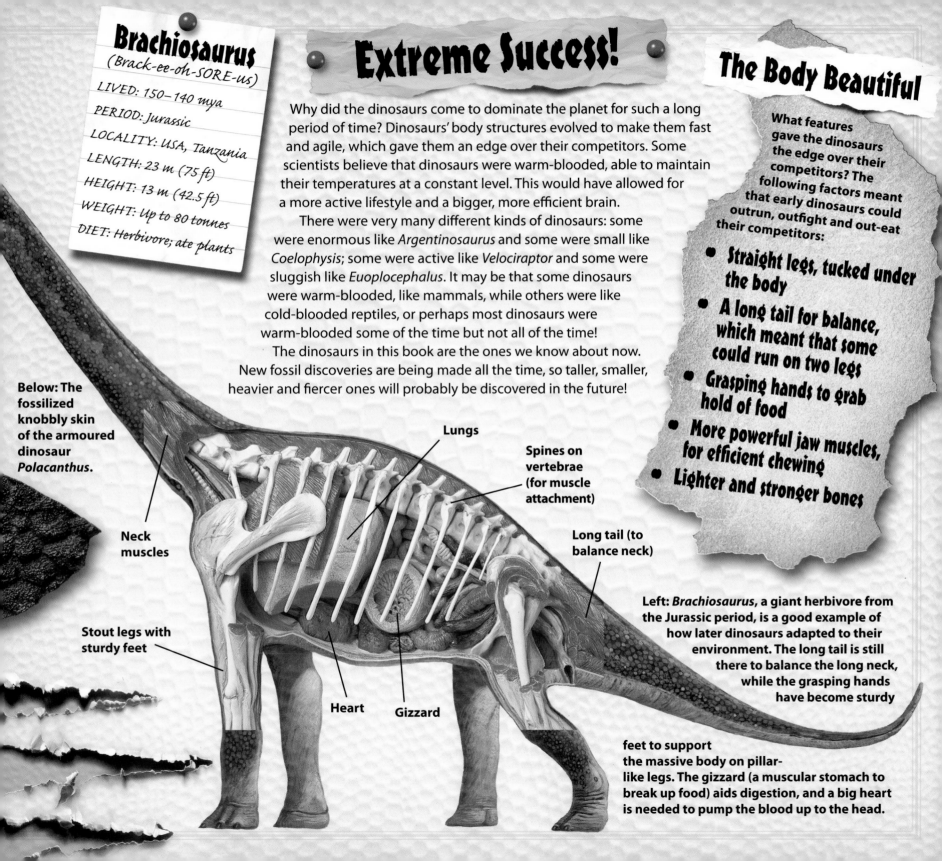

## Brachiosaurus
(Brack-ee-oh-SORE-us)

LIVED: 150–140 mya

PERIOD: Jurassic

LOCALITY: USA, Tanzania

LENGTH: 23 m (75 ft)

HEIGHT: 13 m (42.5 ft)

WEIGHT: Up to 80 tonnes

DIET: Herbivore; ate plants

Why did the dinosaurs come to dominate the planet for such a long period of time? Dinosaurs' body structures evolved to make them fast and agile, which gave them an edge over their competitors. Some scientists believe that dinosaurs were warm-blooded, able to maintain their temperatures at a constant level. This would have allowed for a more active lifestyle and a bigger, more efficient brain.

There were very many different kinds of dinosaurs: some were enormous like *Argentinosaurus* and some were small like *Coelophysis*; some were active like *Velociraptor* and some were sluggish like *Euoplocephalus*. It may be that some dinosaurs were warm-blooded, like mammals, while others were like cold-blooded reptiles, or perhaps most dinosaurs were warm-blooded some of the time but not all of the time!

The dinosaurs in this book are the ones we know about now. New fossil discoveries are being made all the time, so taller, smaller, heavier and fiercer ones will probably be discovered in the future!

## The Body Beautiful

What features gave the dinosaurs the edge over their competitors? The following factors meant that early dinosaurs could outrun, outfight and out-eat their competitors:

- **Straight legs, tucked under the body**
- **A long tail for balance, which meant that some could run on two legs**
- **Grasping hands to grab hold of food**
- **More powerful jaw muscles, for efficient chewing**
- **Lighter and stronger bones**

**Below: The fossilized knobbly skin of the armoured dinosaur *Polacanthus*.**

**Neck muscles**

**Lungs**

**Spines on vertebrae (for muscle attachment)**

**Long tail (to balance neck)**

**Stout legs with sturdy feet**

**Heart**

**Gizzard**

**Left: *Brachiosaurus*, a giant herbivore from the Jurassic period, is a good example of how later dinosaurs adapted to their environment. The long tail is still there to balance the long neck, while the grasping hands have become sturdy feet to support the massive body on pillar-like legs. The gizzard (a muscular stomach to break up food) aids digestion, and a big heart is needed to pump the blood up to the head.**

# Old TIMERS

## Earth, but not as we know it . . .

During the Triassic period, the Earth consisted of one giant land mass, a huge supercontinent called Pangaea. Throughout the Triassic the climate was dry and warm, and because there were no large inland seas or polar ice-caps the temperatures were pretty constant. At this time there were no flowering plants. In the drier parts there were conifer trees like redwoods, cypresses and monkey puzzles, as well as less familiar plants like cycads and podocarps. In moister places and near rivers there were tree ferns, club mosses and horsetails.

**Right: Fossil finds reveal that *Plateosaurus* was the largest early plant-eating dinosaur.**

In 1998, COELOPHYSIS, one of the earliest dinosaurs, took a trip into space! A skull was taken on board the space shuttle ENDEAVOR.

It may be that in these dry and hot conditions, the early dinosaurs' reptilian waterproof skin was better at preventing them from drying out than the fur-covered hide of the early mammals. Whatever the reason, they came to dominate – mammals had to wait for nearly 150 million years for their chance to shine!

## The First Dinosaurs

The first dinosaurs appeared in the late Triassic period, 230 to 225 million years ago. We've already seen how the basic design of the dinosaurs helped them to become successful. Apart from their mobility and speed, what might have given them the edge? Why did dinosaurs beat other animals in the race to the top?

**Right: All continents were once joined to form a single land mass, Pangaea.**

## Moving Continents

During the Triassic period Earth's land mass was very unlike today. Instead of several continents separated by oceans, there was one enormous supercontinent, called Pangaea. During the next 150 million years or so, this land mass gradually split into the continents we know now. Towards the end of the Jurassic period, the northern part of Pangaea, consisting of North America and Asia, had drifted away from the southern part. They formed two new supercontinents – Laurasia in the north and Gondwana in the south – and were separated by the Tethys Ocean. By the end of the Cretaceous period, the positions of the continents were similar to what they are today.

## Lean and Mean

*Coelophysis* is one of the best-known examples of an early dinosaur, and many specimens have been found. About 3 m (10 ft) long, they were lean and mean, fast two-legged meat-eaters. They used grasping claws to capture their victims, and sharp, pointed teeth to devour them. Their teeth would not have been much good at chewing: *Coelophysis* swallowed its prey in bleeding chunks.

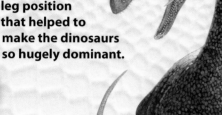

Right: *Coelophysis*, a well-known early dinosaur, shows off the upright leg position that helped to make the dinosaurs so hugely dominant.

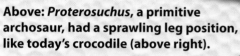

Above: *Proterosuchus*, a primitive archosaur, had a sprawling leg position, like today's crocodile (above right).

Above right: *Euparkeria* had "semi-improved" legs, more upright than those of *Proterosuchus*. The modern-day Komodo dragon (above left) has the same leg position.

## Body Perfect

What do we know about the evolution of the first dinosaurs? We cannot be sure which species of reptiles gave rise to them, but it is likely that an early archosaur, such as *Trilophosaurus*, gave rise to an animal with "semi-improved" legs, rather like *Euparkeria*. This little reptile usually sprawled on its belly, but could run on its hind legs. The next stage would be the evolution of "true" dinosaurs, with straight legs underneath the body, like the early *Herrerasaurus* and *Eoraptor*.

Large prosauropods such as *Plateosaurus* appeared around the same time and became very plentiful. These plant-eaters grew to 8 m (26 ft) in length, and were tall enough to browse among the trees and reach food that smaller dinosaurs could not. Inside their barrel-like bodies were enormously long guts, which contained microbes to ferment the tough Triassic vegetation. This trend was later taken to extremes when herds of the descendants of *Plateosaurus*, sauropods such as *Diplodocus* and *Brachiosaurus*, roamed the Jurassic plains. Finally, being big helped keep prosauropods safe from predators. Earth was now poised for the explosion of dinosaur variety that was to take place in the Jurassic period.

### Coelophysis
(SEEL-oh-FIE-sis))

LIVED: 225–220 mya

PERIOD: Triassic

LOCALITY: USA

LENGTH: 3 m (10 ft)

DIET: Carnivore; ate smaller animals

## Improved Legs

The synapsids had legs that stuck out sideways from the body, just as modern lizards' legs do today. However, the dinosaurs had their legs tucked in beneath the body, meaning that they could stand upright and move quickly, and also breathe more easily. This design feature was one of the most important reasons for the dinosaurs' dominance.

**IMPROVED HIPS:** Hips were strengthened by the joining of some of the hip vertebrae.

**IMPROVED THIGHS:** The head of the thigh bone turned inwards to slot into a strong hip socket.

**IMPROVED KNEES AND ANKLES:** These each had a simple hinge joint, which made them stronger.

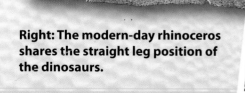

Right: The modern-day rhinoceros shares the straight leg position of the dinosaurs.

# Micro MONSTERS

## The Smallest Dinosaurs

Although many dinosaurs were enormous, some were tiny. Because their bones were small and fragile, they didn't fossilize very easily, and only a few of these small species are well-known.

Scientists found a COMPSOGNATHUS fossil with the bones of an even smaller COMPSOGNATHUS in its stomach cavity. Was this tiny dinosaur a cannibal?

Far left: A tiny *Mussaurus* skeleton, the smallest ever found.

Left: *Microraptor* takes the crown for smallest dinosaur.

## The Smallest of the Small

The tiniest dinosaur ever found was a fossil named *Mussaurus*, or "Mouse Lizard". It was just 18 cm (7 in) and was thought to be the smallest species of dinosaur. However, scientists now believe it to be the skeleton of a baby prosauropod – in time it might have grown to reach a weight of more than 120 kg (265 lb)!

A better candidate for smallest dinosaur is *Microraptor*, discovered in China. It lived in the Cretaceous period and was only 55–75 cm (22–30 in) long. Not only did it have feathers, but it had large flight feathers on both pairs of legs and big feathers on its tail. It seems likely that it spent its time scrambling in trees, jumping and gliding from branch to branch using both pairs of legs. Some scientists believe it may have flapped both pairs of wings, making it an early flying experiment.

## A Miniature Meat-eater

One of the best-known tiny dinosaurs is *Compsognathus*, a nimble chicken-sized dinosaur from the Jurassic period. *Compsognathus* was beautifully adapted to catching small animals such as lizards and insects. Lightly built with hollow bones, its neck was long and flexible, and it could run quickly on its hind legs, using its tail as a balancing rod. The fingers had strong claws, it had big eyes and its nostrils were at the tip of a long tapering nose. This suggests it had a heightened sense of smell for sniffing out prey. The jaws weren't very strong, but they could clamp shut quickly to impale a victim on its small, sharp teeth.

# Mini Dinosaurs

**Right and below:** Dinosaur eggs were amazingly small considering how large the dinosaurs inside would become. The "mini" dinosaurs that hatched from them would have grown at a very fast rate indeed.

**Left:** A well-preserved fossil of *Compsognathus*, the tiny Jurassic meat-eater.

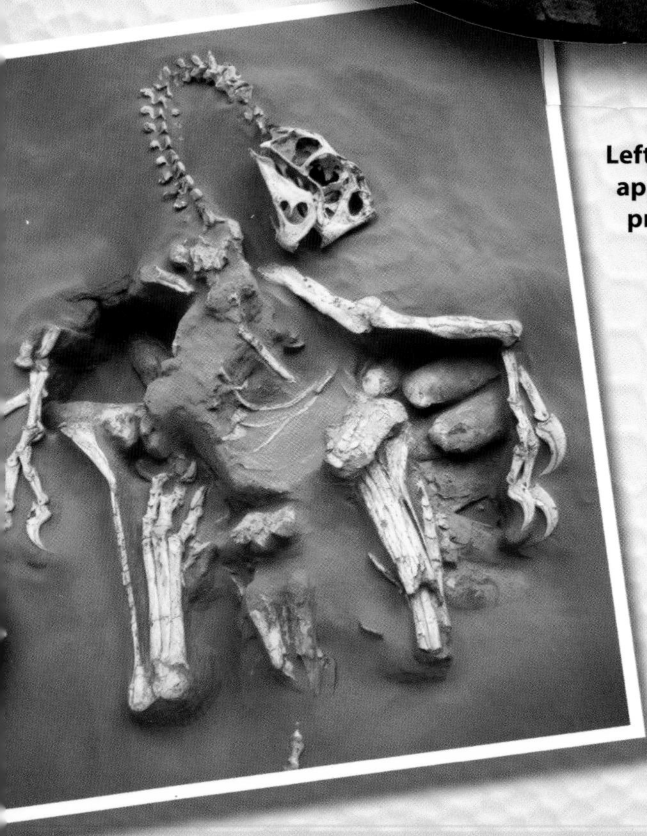

It is not surprising that the discoverers of the *Mussaurus* fossil thought at first that it was a new species of dinosaur, but it was actually a baby! It would have grown up to become a prosauropod plant-eating dinosaur, rather like *Riojasaurus*. Even large sauropods laid surprisingly small eggs. A 30-m (100-ft) long female might lay eggs 30 cm (1 ft) long and 25 cm (10 in) wide – just think how tiny the baby would be compared to the adults!

It is now known that young dinosaurs grew rapidly. Eggs came in all shapes and sizes, and had hard, brittle shells. A few fossilized eggs have contained babies' bones. Fossilized eggs, embryos and mud nests help us to learn about the dinosaurs and their way of life, from growth and size to social organization.

**Left: This *Oviraptor* appears to have died protecting its eggs.**

## Microraptor
(MY-crow-RAP-tor)

LIVED: 130–122 mya

PERIOD: Cretaceous

LOCALITY: China

LENGTH: 55–75 cm (22–30 in)

DIET: Carnivore; ate small animals

**Above:** Scientists believe that *Microraptor* jumped and glided from tree to tree.

If, as most paleontologists agree, birds are descended from the dinosaurs, then the prize for the smallest-ever dinosaur would go to the bee hummingbird found in tropical America. At just 5 cm (2 in) long, its body is the same size as a bumblebee!

# Colossal Plant-eaters

The heaviest (and probably the tallest) sauropod that we can be certain of was *Brachiosaurus*, weighing up to 80 tonnes and 12–13 m (39–43 ft) high. The longest complete skeleton we know of is *Diplodocus*, measuring 28 m (92 ft). Why were the sauropods so huge? One reason is because the bigger you are, the less likely you are to get eaten by a predator. Another advantage of being big is that you can find lots of plants at heights that cannot be reached by smaller dinosaurs. Sauropods were built for strength, not speed. Their thick legs needed to support massive shoulder bones and huge hips, and this meant that they moved very slowly.

 At up to 80 tonnes, **BRACHIOSAURUS** was 80,000 times the weight of **MICRORAPTOR**, the smallest dinosaur.

Above: The fossilized tracks of a massive sauropod, found in Bolivia.

# Super HEAVY

## The Largest Dinosaurs

The largest land animals that ever lived were certainly the dinosaurs, but nobody can be sure which of them was the largest. This is because some of the bits of skeleton we have are just that: pieces of larger bones. What we do know is that the largest dinosaurs were the plant-eating sauropods. They had enormous barrel-shaped bodies with an extremely long tail and neck and a tiny head.

## Colossal Contenders

Some sauropods may have been even bigger than *Brachiosaurus* and *Diplodocus*. The longest neck vertebra ever found was 1.2 m (4 ft), suggesting that its owner, *Sauroposeidon*, was a serious rival. Better fossils of *Argentinosaurus* and *Supersaurus* suggest that these two may have reached lengths of 40 m (131 ft). However, possibly the biggest of all was a giant called *Amphicoelias*. Only part of one bone was discovered, and then lost. Some scientists have calculated that this dinosaur was up to 60 m (197 ft) long and weighed up to a colossal 150 tonnes – as heavy as 25 elephants!

**DIPLODOCUS** was the longest of the land dinosaurs but not the heaviest. Much of its length was taken up by its incredible whip-like tail.

### Diplodocus
(Di-PLOD-o-kus)

LIVED: 155–145 mya

PERIOD: Jurassic

LOCALITY: USA

LENGTH: 28 m (92 ft)

WEIGHT: 10–16 tonnes

DIET: Herbivore; ate conifers and other leaves

# WEIGHTS

## Gigantic Flesh-eaters

Above: The massive skull of *Carcharodontosaurus*, a giant meat-eater from North Africa. Seen next to a man's skull, it is clear that this dinosaur would have had no trouble in swallowing a human whole!

Which was the biggest carnivore? Unfortunately, just as with the herbivores, some of the likely candidates are known from only a few bones, so we can't say for certain. *Spinosaurus* was perhaps the longest (but not the heaviest or bulkiest) meat-eater at 18m (59 ft) long. *Tyrannosaurus*, long considered the largest meat-eater at around 12.5 m (41 ft) long, was pushed into second place in 1994 when a huge and almost complete skeleton was unearthed by an amateur fossil-hunter. Named *Giganotosaurus*, this powerful monster may have reached a length of just over 14 m (46 ft). It had enormous jaws with 20-cm (8-in) serrated teeth in a 6-ft (1.8-m) long skull. These two dinosaurs were also the heaviest meat-eaters. Other contenders for biggest carnivore are *Carcharodontosaurus* and *Tyrannotitan*, both relatives of *Giganotosaurus*.

Above: The amazing length of *Diplodocus* has led scientists to question how it moved and fed. Some believe it could raise itself up on its massive hind legs to reach high trees.

Right: Perhaps the largest predator ever to stalk the Earth, *Giganotosaurus* terrorized the South American landscape around 90 million years ago.

## Giganotosaurus
(Gig-an-oh-toe-SORE-us)

LIVED: 112–90 mya

PERIOD: Cretaceous

LOCALITY: Argentina

LENGTH: 14 m (46 ft)

WEIGHT: 7–8 tonnes

DIET: Carnivore; ate plant eating dinosaurs

# Tough GUYS

Left: *Gastonia* was like an armoured tank. Predators would have needed to flip it over to expose its soft belly.

## The Best-protected Dinosaurs

Two groups of dinosaurs protected themselves from predators by reinforcing their bodies and tails with spines or armour, or both. These were the stegosaurs and the ankylosaurs.

*Huayangosaurus* was one of the earliest stegosaurs and may have given rise to later species such as *Kentrosaurus* and *Stegosaurus*. It was about 4 m (13 ft) long and had a double row of narrow, pointed, bony plates protecting its neck and back. A pair of long spikes protected its hip area, and there were two pairs of spikes at the end of its tail: it could swing these round to defend itself. *Stegosaurus* was much bigger. Its thick skin was encrusted with bones and the two pairs of spikes at the end of its tail protected it from carnivores such as *Allosaurus*, but because it was so much taller than *Huayangosaurus*, it may not have needed to protect its back so much, and the sharply pointed plates there became huge and flat like enormous paving stones.

The very eyelids of EUOPLOCEPHALUS were part of its armour. Made of bone, they shielded the eyes from attacking claws.

## Armed to the Teeth

The real tough guys were the armoured dinosaurs, or ankylosaurs. There were several species but they all relied heavily on armour, with sheets of bone protecting the skull, neck and back, just as bony plates protect crocodiles' backs today. The body was often covered with horns and spikes. When attacked by a predator, their strategy was a combination of active and passive defence. A spiky species such as *Gastonia* would squat on the ground and rely on its armour, rather like today's armadillo; a club-tailed species like *Euoplocephalus* would try to disable its attacker with a blow from its tail. Nowadays, a porcupine will charge an attacking lion (backwards!), trying to spike it.

**Left: A spiky porcupine deters a hungry lion.**

STEGOSAURUS had a brain the size of a walnut! What it was missing in brains, it made up for in brawn.

Above: *Allosaurus*, a powerful predator, would have risked a lash from the potentially lethal *Stegosaurus* tail in its search for food.

Above: *Stegosaurus* would have swung its spiked tail like a club in an attempt to drive away predators.

## Stegosaurus
### (Steg-UH-sore-us)

LIVED: 155– 145 mya

PERIOD: Jurassic

LOCALITY: USA

LENGTH: 9 m (29.5 ft)

DIET: A herbivore; ate low-growing plants

## Tails of Defence

Some dinosaurs had devastating counter-attacking weapons: their tails. *Stegosaurus* had four tail spikes which were approximately 90 cm (3 ft) long. The tail of *Euoplocephalus* (shown right) was around 2.5 m (8 ft) in length, and ended with a massive club composed of two fused bones weighing up to 30 kg (66 lb). A single blow to the legs from this deadly structure could crush bones, fatally disabling a predator such as *Tyrannosaurus*.

## The Plates of STEGOSAURUS

What were the bony plates on the back of STEGOSAURUS used for? There are several possibilities:

**Defence:** The plates were too far up on the dinosaur's back to be much use as armour. However, they were thin and lined with blood vessels, and if suddenly filled with blood, the flushing plates might have frightened off predators.

**2. Temperature regulation:** The sun would warm the blood flowing through the plates, which was then pumped through the body. When the dinosaur became too hot, it could turn away from the sun, thus cooling the plates.

**3. Courtship display:** The female may have flushed her plates with blood to show that she was ready to mate, just as female chimpanzees flush their bottoms.

**4. Defence against rivals:** Just as male deer use their antlers to intimidate rivals, *Stegosaurus* may have used its flushing back plates to warn off rivals.

**5. Species recognition:** Both sexes may have used their back plates to identify themselves to each other as members of the same species.

# Sprinters and PLODDERS

Fossilized skeletons provide some clues to the speeds of different dinosaurs; other clues come from fossilized dinosaur tracks. One problem in estimating dinosaur speeds is that most fossil tracks show them strolling rather than sprinting!

## Built for Speed

Most scientists agree that the fastest dinosaurs were two-legged. Fast dinosaurs had several features in common, such as light bones, streamlined bodies and long lower limbs. These features were possessed by the ornithomimids, or "ostrich dinosaurs", such as *Gallimimus* and *Struthiomimus*. Like ostriches, they ran on two legs, had a toothless beak and were omnivores, feeding on plants and insects. Unlike ostriches, they were featherless, had long tails for balance and grasping arms. Ostriches can run at speeds of up to 70 kph (43 mph); *Gallimimus*, the largest ornithomimid, might well have been as fast.

**Above:** *Velociraptor* was not as fast as a cheetah, but, like hunting cats, it combined speed and agility with vicious teeth and claws.

**Right:** The long, powerful hind limbs of *Gallimimus* were designed for sprinting.

### Gallimimus
(Gal-lee-MY-mus)

LIVED: 74–70 mya

PERIOD: Cretaceous

LOCALITY: Mongolia

LENGTH: 5.5 m (18 ft)

DIET: Omnivore; ate plants and small animals

## Swift and Deadly

*Velociraptor* ("speedy thief") had a light, streamlined body, long "running legs" and a stiff tail that acted as a counter-balance when sprinting, allowing the dinosaur to turn quickly if necessary. Like modern-day hunting cats, *Velociraptor* combined speed and agility with needle-sharp teeth and killer claws. Some scientists think these dinosaurs hunted in packs, perhaps preying on dinosaurs much larger than themselves. It is estimated that a human being could have been torn apart in under 30 seconds by a pack of *Velociraptors*!

Were any dinosaur meat-eaters likely to have been as fast as the ostrich dinosaurs? A good candidate is *Velociraptor*. It had to catch its prey by running it down and had the features of a sprinter: long slim legs, a stiff tail for balance and a streamlined body. Other fast dinosaurs were *Hypsilophodon* and the little Triassic *Coelophysis*, both plant-eaters designed for a quick getaway. But which dinosaur was the fastest of all? It's not possible to be sure, but it was probably *Gallimimus*. Animals that have only one chance to escape death by running are usually faster than those that can afford to have several chances to catch their dinner.

# The Plodders

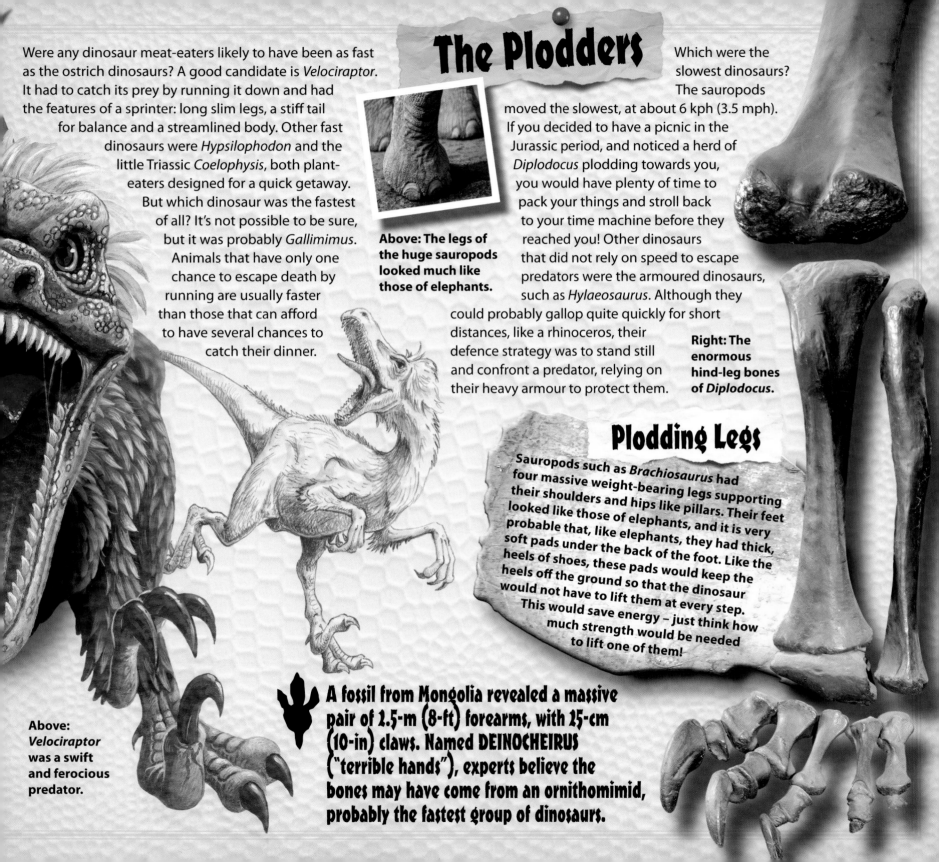

**Above: The legs of the huge sauropods looked much like those of elephants.**

Which were the slowest dinosaurs? The sauropods moved the slowest, at about 6 kph (3.5 mph). If you decided to have a picnic in the Jurassic period, and noticed a herd of *Diplodocus* plodding towards you, you would have plenty of time to pack your things and stroll back to your time machine before they reached you! Other dinosaurs that did not rely on speed to escape predators were the armoured dinosaurs, such as *Hylaeosaurus*. Although they could probably gallop quite quickly for short distances, like a rhinoceros, their defence strategy was to stand still and confront a predator, relying on their heavy armour to protect them.

**Right: The enormous hind-leg bones of *Diplodocus*.**

## Plodding Legs

Sauropods such as *Brachiosaurus* had four massive weight-bearing legs supporting their shoulders and hips like pillars. Their feet looked like those of elephants, and it is very probable that, like elephants, they had thick, soft pads under the back of the foot. Like the heels of shoes, these pads would keep the heels off the ground so that the dinosaur would not have to lift them at every step. This would save energy – just think how much strength would be needed to lift one of them!

**Above: *Velociraptor* was a swift and ferocious predator.**

A fossil from Mongolia revealed a massive pair of 2.5-m (8-ft) forearms, with 25-cm (10-in) claws. Named DEINOCHEIRUS ("terrible hands"), experts believe the bones may have come from an ornithomimid, probably the fastest group of dinosaurs.

# ODDBALLS

Dinosaurs reigned supreme on land, but they did not succeed in the water or the air. In prehistoric seas, familiar marine animals such as corals and fish existed alongside outlandish marine reptiles such as plesiosaurs and ichthyosaurs. The masters of the air were the pterosaurs, flying reptiles closely related to the dinosaurs.

**Above: The mighty *Quetzalcoatlus* was king of Cretaceous skies.**

## A Giant Glider

The biggest pterosaur, in fact the largest flying creature of all time, was the late Cretaceous *Quetzalcoatlus*, named after the serpent god of the Aztecs. With a wingspan up to 12 m (39 ft), the size of a small plane, it had hollow bones and weighed just 100 kg (220 lb). Unlike birds it had no feathers, but could fold its wings and had a claw on its thumb, like a bat. It may have slept like a bat, too, hanging upside-down by its feet. *Quetzalcoatlus* was not an agile flier, relying instead on soaring and gliding. On the end of a long neck was a 2-m (6.5-ft) long head, most of it a toothless beak used to catch invertebrates such as crabs and molluscs, or possibly fish.

## Quetzalcoatlus
*(Kwet-zal-co-art-lus)*

LIVED: 84–65 mya

PERIOD: Cretaceous

LOCALITY: USA

WINGSPAN: 12 m (39 ft)

WEIGHT: 100 kg (220 lb)

DIET: Carnivore; ate invertebrates and fish

**Right: A superbly complete *Pterodactylus* fossil.**

## Masters of the Air

The pterosaurs, or winged reptiles, lived alongside dinosaurs throughout the Triassic, Jurassic and Cretaceous periods. Their wings consisted of a membrane of reinforced skin stretching from a very long fourth finger to the body, as far as the back legs. Flying animals need extremely lightweight bodies; the pterosaurs had hollow bones, even thinner than those of birds, and were probably warm-blooded. The first pterosaur ever discovered was *Pterodactylus*; it is also the earliest one known and lived in the Triassic period, 225 million years ago. The South American *Pterodaustro* holds the record for number of teeth, with between 500 and 1,000! It probably used these to filter-feed on plankton, like flamingos do. The smallest pterosaur was the Jurassic sparrow-sized *Anurognathus*.

# Monsters of the Deep

## Liopleurodon
(LIE-oh-PLOO-ro-don)

LIVED: 160–155 mya
PERIOD: Jurassic
LOCALITY: UK, France
LENGTH: 25 m (82 ft)
WEIGHT: 100–150 tonnes
DIET: Carnivore; ate any large living thing

Under water, the greatest aquatic predator was the plesiosaur *Liopleurodon*. Plesiosaurs breathed air and used paddle-like limbs to swim. *Liopleurodon* lived during the Jurassic and may have weighed up to 150 tonnes; it reached 25 m (82 ft) in length – its head was 5 m (16 ft) long! The position of the nostrils on the skull suggests that, like modern-day sharks, it may have found its food by smell. It would have eaten giant turtles, ammonites (early relatives of the squid) and other plesiosaurs. The ichthyosaurs were giant reptiles that resembled fish and dolphins. Among the biggest was *Shonisaurus*, which was at least 15 m (49 ft) long. This reptile swam like a shark, using its forked tail to propel it as fast as 40 kph (25 mph) to catch its prey of ammonites, fish and even the odd pterosaur.

**OPHTHALMOSAURUS was an ichthyosaur with enormous eyes, 10 cm (4 in) across! These helped it to spot its prey in the deep, dark ocean.**

Left: The 110 million-year-old skull of a *Sarcosuchus* crocodile dwarfs the skull of the modern-day Orinoco crocodile.

Above: *Liopleurodon*, perhaps the largest predator Earth has ever seen.

# Extreme Crocodiles!

**There is evidence that SHONISAURUS fed on pterosaurs alongside its usual prey of fish and ammonites. Nobody knows how this aquatic creature managed to capture these flying reptiles!**

Crocodiles are archosaurs and are related to dinosaurs. *Deinosuchus* and *Sarcosuchus* both lived in the Cretaceous period and are the biggest crocodiles ever found. *Deinosuchus*, with a skull nearly 2 m (6.5 ft) long and teeth to match, was well-equipped to seize hadrosaurs and even large carnivores that approached the water's edge. It would have behaved like today's crocodiles, invisibly approaching its prey and then lunging out to grab and pull it into the water.

# Ferocious BEASTS

## Spinosaurus
### (SPINE-oh-SORE-us)

LIVED: 95–70 mya

PERIOD: Cretaceous

LOCALITY: North Africa

LENGTH: 18 m (59 ft)

DIET: A carnivore; ate large fish and other dinosaurs

**Above: This huge _Baryonyx_ fossil claw bone (shown lifesize) was found in 1983 in a clay pit in Surrey, England.**

**Below: _Spinosaurus_ had crocodile-like jaws for grabbing its prey.**

Among the dinosaurs were some of the most ferocious and terrifying creatures to ever walk the Earth. Some of them, such as TYRANNOSAURUS REX, grew to huge proportions and used their size to overpower their victims. Smaller carnivores were just as deadly and often hunted in packs, combining speed with a lethal array of weapons, such as razor-sharp fangs, giant hook-like claws and very powerful jaws.

## The Deadly Spinosaurus

One of the most ferocious dinosaurs that ever existed, _Spinosaurus_ was also one of the most spectacular. Along its back were bony spines, 1.8 m (5.9 ft) in length, that supported a large sail of skin. At up to 18 m (59 ft) long, it was probably longer and certainly more agile than _Tyrannosaurus_ or _Giganotosaurus_, though it was lighter in weight.

Like the clawed dinosaurs, it walked and ran on two legs, but unlike them it probably hunted alone, using its size and ambush tactics to catch its prey. Its 2 m- (6.5 ft-) long skull had crocodile-like jaws with long, sharp teeth, but unlike _Tyrannosaurus_ and the clawed dinosaurs, its teeth were not serrated. As with today's crocodiles, its prey probably consisted of large fish, but it would also have used its enormous jaws to disable and kill other large dinosaurs. Clamping its jaws into the back or sides of its prey, this dinosaur could then tear off large chunks of flesh, or hang on until the animal was disabled before settling down to eat it.

# Terrible Claws!

## Deinonychus
### (Die-NON-ee-kus)

LIVED: 110 mya

PERIOD: Cretaceous

LOCALITY: USA

LENGTH: 3 m (10 ft)

DIET: A carnivore; ate large herbivores when hunting in packs

The clawed dinosaurs, such as *Velociraptor*, *Deinonychus* and *Utahraptor*, were lethal hunters. By dinosaur standards they were small, but they made up for this with their claws, great speed and their method of hunting in packs, like wolves or lions. *Deinonychus* (Greek for "terrible claw") had three normal-sized claws on each of its hind feet, and one, on the second toe, that was enlarged to form a deadly, flesh-penetrating, muscle-ripping blade – in the case of *Utahraptor* this was 30 cm (12 in) long. When these dinosaurs ran on their hind legs, this claw was held clear of the ground, but when they caught up with their prey, the claw swung down to cut and tear. The dinosaur would then hold the struggling victim down with strong, three-fingered hands, while bringing one of its powerful back legs up to kick it to the ground and disembowel it. Finally, the dinosaur's strong jaws, packed with backward-pointing serrated teeth, tore into the prey, and the feeding frenzy began.

Bony struts reinforced the tail of DEINONYCHUS so that it could hold its tail still when running. This helped it to balance.

Below: A *Tenontosaurus* is attacked by a savage pack of *Deinonychus*. These fearsome predators had terrible curved claws for slashing through tough skin and muscle.

# The Longest and the TALLEST

Above: Like the modern-day giraffe, *Brachiosaurus* was built to feed from high trees.

## Tall Stories

The tallest living mammal is the giraffe, which can reach 6 m (19.5 ft) high. *Brachiosaurus*, standing at up to 13 m (42.5 ft), was the tallest dinosaur. Its fore legs were longer than its hind legs, and it held its neck upright: these features suggest that, like a giraffe, it fed from the tops of trees. If *Sauroposeidon*, an immensely long-necked dinosaur, had been built to stand upright like *Brachiosaurus*, it could have been 18 m (59 ft) tall. Although *Brachiosaurus* and its relatives held their heads high, it is likely that the long necks of most giant sauropods were held horizontally. This would allow the head to cover great areas of low-growing plants without the dinosaur using too much energy. Some scientists think that *Sauroposeidon* was such an example, meaning it was very long rather than very tall!

**Right: The enormously long tail of *Apatosaurus* counterbalanced its very long neck.**

**Left: The upright *Brachiosaurus* is the tallest dinosaur that scientists can be sure of.**

## Incredible Necks and Tails

The sauropods were not only the heaviest dinosaurs, but also the tallest, and had the longest necks and tails. Most sauropods held their necks horizontally rather than upright. Not all scientists agree, but perhaps dinosaurs like MAMENCHISAURUS could rear up on their back legs, allowing them to feed from treetops.

## A Cracking Tail

The record for the longest tail, at 13 m (42.5 ft), is held by *Diplodocus*. If, as many scientists think, *Diplodocus* stood on its hind legs to reach the treetops, the tail could have helped to steady the body. It may also have been used like a whip in defence against predators such as *Allosaurus*. However, the final two metres of the tail were very thin, not much more than 30 mm (1 in – striking heavy predators would probably have damaged it! It has been calculated that the tip of the tail could have been moved at supersonic speeds, producing a loud cracking noise that might have been used to deter enemies. *Diplodocus* might also have moved its tail to communicate with members of the same species.

# Reaching for the Stars

It is likely that other sauropods, such as *Diplodocus* and *Mamenchisaurus*, could reach just as high or even higher than *Brachiosaurus*, by rearing up on their hind legs. The hind legs of *Diplodocus*, unlike those of *Brachiosaurus*, were bigger than its fore legs. This means that its centre of gravity was further back, and this could have allowed it to rear up while the tail steadied it behind. Bony chevrons on the bases of the tail vertebrae may have been there to stop the blood vessels from getting crushed when the tail pressed upon the ground. The neck was 8 m (26 ft) long, and its tiny head could easily have reached the treetops.

**Above: A fossilized vertebra from the sauropod *Barosaurus*. Probably four fifths of this dinosaur's length was neck and tail!**

**Right: The gerenuk, a modern-day African antelope, rears up on its back legs to feed. Sauropods like *Mamenchisaurus* may well have fed in the same way.**

In 2005, scientists announced the discovery of a stumpy-necked sauropod! BRACHYTRACHELOPAN had a neck shorter than its backbone, making it the shortest sauropod neck on record.

The record for the longest neck-to-body ratio is held by a sauropod called ERKETU. This dinosaur's neck, at 8 m (26 ft) long, was twice the length of its body!

## A Neck to Die For

Although it couldn't reach as high as *Diplodocus*, the Chinese dinosaur *Mamenchisaurus* had a neck that was nearly 14 m (46 ft) long, the longest we are sure about. The neck consisted of 19 bones; these were hollow and lightweight, making it possible for *Mamenchisaurus* to support its amazing length. *Sauroposeidon* may have had a longer neck still. Although only four fossil bones have ever been found belonging to this dinosaur, they are all neck vertebrae and they are each an incredible 1.2 m (4 ft) long. If *Sauroposeidon* was able to rear up on its hind legs, it may have been able to reach higher than any other dinosaur.

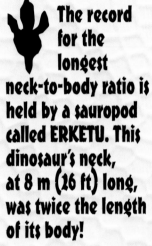

*Left: Mamenchisaurus takes the prize for the longest neck.*

## Mamenchisaurus
### (Mah-MEN-chi-SORE-us)

LIVED: 155–145 mya

PERIOD: Jurassic

LOCALITY: China

LENGTH: 24 m (80 ft)

DIET: A herbivore; ate high-growing plants

# Master-MINDS

Dinosaurs have never had much of a reputation for intelligence. There is no doubt that many dinosaurs got by with very little brain power, but just as with mammals living today, some groups were smarter than others.

## Clever is as Clever Does

There are two main ways of finding out how intelligent an extinct animal was: scientists can look at its way of life and see how complicated this was, or they can measure the animal's brain relative to its body size. Animals that lead complicated lives are usually more intelligent than animals that lead simple lives. The sauropods were so enormous that they didn't need to worry about predators, and they were the least intelligent of the dinosaurs. Smaller herbivores such as *Stegosaurus* required very little brain power to find their food, but they needed to be able to defend themselves against predators. The horned dinosaurs seem to have had a more social life, probably living in herds and needing to communicate with each other. *Triceratops* was a little brighter than *Stegosaurus*, but still probably relied on its armour for survival. Plant-eating dinosaurs without armour, such as *Iguanodon*, lived fairly complex lives in herds, and relied more on communication and reacting quickly. Large carnivores such as *Tyrannosaurus* needed to find their food, and then catch and kill it. They had forward-facing eyes, or binocular vision, so that they could judge distances; a bigger brain was needed for these complicated activities. Fast-running carnivores such as *Velociraptor* needed even more intelligence; they had to be able to communicate with other members of the pack. At the top of the heap would be the smaller carnivores that stalked and chased their prey, such as the troodonts.

**Above:
The skull of *Diplodocus*. The massive saurpods were pretty low on brain power!**

## A Question of Size?

The brain itself doesn't fossilize, so scientists have to estimate its size by making a cast of the inside of the skull. Bigger animals have larger brains than smaller animals, so you need to compare the brain with the size of the dinosaur to get some idea of its intelligence. When you compare the intelligence of different dinosaurs using this method, you tend to get the same result as you would by looking at their lifestyles – the dim sauropods come bottom of the class and the brighter, smaller carnivores come top.

## Troodon
(TRUE-oh-don)

LIVED: 75–70 mya

PERIOD: Cretaceous

LOCALITY: Canada and USA

LENGTH: 2.5 m (8 ft)

DIET: Carnivore; ate small animals

The back edge of *Pachycephalosaurus*'s massive skull was covered with bony knobs and there were short bony spikes on top of the snout. It had very small, sharp, ridged teeth that would have made good shredders. *Pachycephalosaurus* probably ate a mixed diet of soft leaves, seeds and fruit, with perhaps the odd insect.

The only part of *Pachycephalosaurus* that has been found is the skull. However, it had smaller relatives, such as *Stegoceras*, and these give us a fairly good idea of what *Pachycephalosaurus* looked like and how it lived. All the evidence from fossils suggests that these dinosaurs used their thick heads for butting. The spine was strengthened with bony rods and the joint between the skull and the neck vertebrae was designed to absorb shock. It used to be thought that the male *Pachycephalosaurus* fought for a mate by ramming a rival's head. However, scientists have since discovered that the skull was not strong enough to withstand this sort of head-to-head shock and it seems more likely that they used their heads to ram predators. Although *Pachycephalosaurus* was probably not very fast, even *Tyrannosaurus* would have been hurt if a dinosaur the length of a large car crashed into its flank head first!

## Fancy Headgear

Many hadrosaurs had tall crests on their heads. The males had bigger crests, which were probably brightly coloured and used for displays to attract females and to threaten other males during courtship. Some of the crests were hollow, and may have been used as resonating chambers to make different loud noises, or "songs". *Parasaurolophus* (above) had perhaps the strangest crest of all: shaped like a trombone and nearly 1.8 m (6 ft) long.

Incredibly, the mighty head belonging to PACHYCEPHALOSAURUS housed a brain not much bigger than an apple!

## Impressing the Ladies

Dinosaurs such as *Pentaceratops* and *Pachycephalosaurus* used their heads for fighting and display. *Oviraptor* and carnivores such as *Ceratosaurus* and *Dilophosaurus* had crests and probably also used them for display. Some dinosaurs used other parts of their bodies. *Heterodontosaurus* males had tusks, like wild boars, while *Spinosaurus* may have used his dorsal crest to attract females or to intimidate other males. *Stegosaurus* may have used his bony plates, and *Deinonychus* his long sickle-claws, for the same reasons.

Above: The skull of *Pachycephalosaurus* had a huge dome of bone.

# Extreme EATERS

Like all animals, dinosaurs needed food for energy. For plant-eaters, the challenge came in getting enough food and breaking it down. The flesh-eaters needed to catch their prey and kill it, or at least stop it from moving. Dinosaurs developed special equipment, from beaks to teeth, to catch and process their food.

Right: Sauropods needed stomach stones to aid digestion.

Above: A fossilized *Protoceratops* skull. These dinosaurs had sharp, toothless beaks for slicing leaves and shoots.

## Heavy-Duty Eating

The heaviest dinosaur, a sauropod such as *Brachiosaurus*, probably needed to eat about a tonne of plants every day! Its little peg-teeth were no good for chewing and its head was no bigger than a horse's, so how did it process all this food? It swallowed stones (gastroliths) which ground together in the gizzard, a muscular stomach, to help break up food; this was very inefficient, so the gut was enormously long to give time for digestion to occur.

The smaller herbivores, such as *Hadrosaurus*, had efficient grinding teeth, while ceratopians such as *Triceratops* used their beaks to slice up tough plant food.

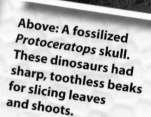

Left: *Oviraptor* was able to use its powerful jaw and "teeth" to crush eggs.

## Grinders, Slicers and Crushers

A duck-billed dinosaur (hadrosaur) such as *Edmontosaurus* used its horn-covered beak to pull in tough plant food, such as bark. Its jaw contained over 1,000 teeth; those on the hinged upper jaw met the lower teeth, then moved past them so that the two rough surfaces rubbed each other, grinding the food.

The horned dinosaurs had sharp, narrow, toothless beaks rather like a parrot's. *Protoceratops* used its beak to slice off tough shoots and leaves; further back in the mouth it had self-sharpening, scissor-like tooth batteries that chopped and sliced food.

*Oviraptor*'s jaws were probably covered with a horny sheath like a bird's beak. Although it had no teeth, there were two knobs that looked a bit like big teeth. These formed a pair of prongs in the roof of the mouth which were used to crush dinosaurs' eggs, and possibly hard fruit or even shellfish.

## Meaty Mouthfuls

Carnivores would single out "easy" prey – the sick, the old or the young. Crashing in at high speed, with mouth wide open, a predator would drive its sharp upper teeth straight into the victim. *Allosaurus* and *Giganotosaurus* would use their arms to hold on to the victim, but *Tyrannosaurus* had tiny arms so it used its powerful neck muscles to rip out flesh with its mouth, swallowing it straight away. *Tyrannosaurus* could easily pulverize tough items such as bones and swallow the fragments. A huge predator like this would need to eat the equivalent of three or four adult *Triceratops* (or 292 adult men!) per year.

Smaller predators were fast runners, and had specialized appendages: *Deinonychus* and *Velociraptor* had lethal, swivelling claws, and most of the others, such as *Coelophysis* and *Troodon*, had grasping hands and binocular vision. It is likely that some species hunted in packs, running down slower dinosaurs. Most of the predators had a well-developed sense of smell.

**Below:** *Tyrannosaurus* would have used its hugely powerful neck and jaws to violently shake its victims to death.

## Dinosaur Droppings

Coprolites, pieces of fossilized dung, can provide useful information about dinosaurs' diets. They may contain items such as seeds, leaves, fish scales, teeth and bits of partially digested bone. Many coprolites are up to 40 cm (16 in) in diameter, and were probably deposited by sauropods like *Diplodocus*.

**Left: Coprolites provide interesting clues as to what dinosaurs ate.**

### Tyrannosaurus
(Tie-ran-OH-sore-us)

LIVED: 75–65 mya

PERIOD: Cretaceous

LOCALITY: USA

LENGTH: 12.5 m (41 ft)

DIET: Carnivore; ate other dinosaurs, alive or dead

## Death by Degrees?

By the end of the Cretaceous period, there were fewer dinosaur species and these were dominated by herbivores such as *Edmontosaurus* and *Triceratops*, and occasional bone-headed dinosaurs like *Pachycephalosaurus*. Ostrich dinosaurs such as *Ornithomimus* roamed the open areas and the sickle-clawed *Troodon* was common. The fearsome *Tyrannosaurus* kept close to the enormous herds of plant-eaters. While the dinosaurs were becoming fewer in variety, mammals were increasing.

The climate was becoming wetter. Perhaps the formation of new rivers and more swamps made it more difficult for the herbivores to reach fresh feeding ranges. If this caused a decline in their numbers, it would have affected the carnivores' food supply and their numbers would also have dropped. However, this does not explain the sudden disappearance not only of the dinosaurs roaming the land but also the reptiles dominating the sea and the pterosaurs cruising the sky.

In addition, ammonites (a type of shellfish) and belemnites (relatives of the squid) and 90 per cent of the plankton also vanished, as did 75 per cent of all other species. On land it was fatal to be longer than a metre or heavier than about 30 kg (66 lb)! What happened so quickly that large land animals had no time to adapt?

### Edmontosaurus
### (Ed-MON-toe-SAWR-us)

LIVED: 76–65 mya

PERIOD: Cretaceous

LOCALITY: Canada

LENGTH: 13 m (42.5 ft)

DIET: Herbivore; ate low-lying plants

# DEATH
## and Extinction

For more than 160 million years the dinosaurs dominated the land, but around 65 million years ago they disappeared completely. Why? Did they decline gradually, or did a single catastrophic event wipe them out forever?

### Farewell to the Dinosaurs

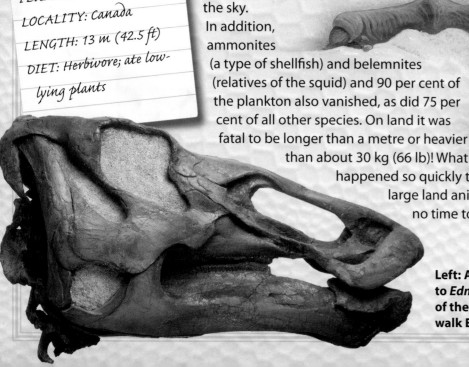

### The Survivors

Apart from birds, the most successful survivors from the dinosaur age were the mammals. In the Cretaceous period most of them were small and obtained their food by catching small invertebrates such as insects or by scavenging. Examples are *Zalambdalestes* from Mongolia or *Megazostrodon* from Lesotho. Both were long-nosed mammals with large eyes and sharp teeth. *Didelphodon*, a marsupial related to opossums, was one of the biggest.

Left: A skull belonging to *Edmontosaurus*, one of the last dinosaurs to walk Earth.

Above (inset): The modern-day elephant shrew eats small invertebrates, as did the mammal survivors from the age of dinosaurs.

Left: *Edmontosaurus* lies dead in the sand.

# The End of an Era

In 1978 an American scientist discovered high levels of an element called iridium in the layer of rock formed at the end of the Cretaceous period, 65 million years ago (the K-T Boundary). Iridium has since been found in more than 50 sites worldwide. It is usually found in cosmic dust from outer space or from the Earth's core when volcanos erupt. Many scientists think it likely that either a large object from outer space, such as a meteorite or asteroid, landed on Earth or a large number of volcanic eruptions occurred at that time, bringing an end to the dinosaurs.

In 1990 scientists discovered a crater measuring 180 km (112 miles) across in Chicxulub, Mexico. The asteroid or comet that caused it would have measured around 10 km (6 miles) across. Was this the catastrophe that wiped out the dinosaurs?

## Apocalypse!

What would have been the effect of a huge asteroid from space, 10 km (6 miles) wide, hitting the Earth at 100,000 kmph (62,000 mph)? Firstly, there would have been a massive blast, destroying everything within 500 km (300 miles). If it had crashed into the sea, gigantic ocean waves (tsunamis) would have smashed into coastlines. A series of volcanic eruptions would have been triggered. Heating of the atmosphere would have occurred, and a huge cloud of vapourized hot debris would have been thrown up. Some would have rained down, causing wildfires and acid rain; the rest would have hidden the sun, creating a global winter of darkness and low temperatures that would destroy plants. Without plants, the herbivores would die; without herbivores, the carnivores would die. The only survivors would have been small scavengers, such as birds and mammals, that could find food from a variety of different sources (including dead dinosaurs).

Right (main image): A huge asteroid hitting Earth would have triggered a series of volcanic eruptions.
Right (inset, top): An artist's impression of the impact that caused the Chicxulub crater.
Right (inset, bottom): An asteroid collision with Earth would have caused giant tsunamis that would have devastated coastal habitats.

# GLOSSARY

**Acid rain** Rain polluted by acid gases that damages many organisms.

**Ammonites** An extinct group of shellfish from the Mesozoic era, related to squid and octopuses.

**Amphibians** Cold-blooded vertebrates that live on land but return to the water to breed, such as frogs and newts.

**Ankylosaurs** Armoured, plant-eating ornithischian dinosaurs.

**Archosaurs** A group of reptiles that includes dinosaurs, pterosaurs, thecodonts and crocodiles.

**Belemnites** An extinct group of molluscs, with an internal shell.

**Binocular vision** Forward-facing eyes that can see three-dimensional pictures, enabling an animal to judge distances.

**Camouflage** Concealment, usually by being coloured like the background.

**Carnivore** A meat-eater.

**Cold-blooded** Having a body temperature that rises and falls with the outside temperature.

**Conifers** A cone-bearing tree such as a yew or pine.

**Continent** A large, continuous body of land, e.g. Africa.

**Coprolite** Fossilized dung.

**Corals** Sea animals, related to sea anemones, with tough outside skeletons, often forming reefs.

**Courtship display** Behaviour used to attract a partner for reproduction.

**Cretaceous period** The third period of the Mesozoic era, lasting from 135 to 65 million years ago.

**Cycads** Squat, palm-like plants, common in the Mesozoic era. Some survive today.

**Dinosaurs** A group of land-living reptiles with an upright stance that lived between 230 and 65 million years ago.

**Embryo** An animal or plant in its earliest stages of development.

**Evolution** The process by which one species gives rise to another by gradual changes over a period of time.

**Extinction** The dying out of a species.

**Ferns** Early non-flowering land plants, common in the Mesozoic era and surviving today.

**Fossil** The preserved remains of a once-living organism.

**Gastroliths** Stomach stones used for grinding food.

**Ginkgo** Also known as the maidenhair tree, with ancestors common in the Mesozoic era.

**Gizzard** The muscular part of the stomach used to grind up food.

**Hadrosaurs** Duck-billed dinosaurs living in the Cretaceous period.

**Herbivore** A plant-eater.

**Horsetails** Primitive non-flowering plants common in the Triassic period and surviving today.

**Ice-caps** Areas of ice covering the North and South Poles.

**Ichthyosaurs** Sea reptiles of the Mesozoic era.

**Invertebrates** Animals without a backbone.

**Iridium** A metal found in meteorites and the Earth's core.

**Jurassic period** The middle period of the Mesozoic era, lasting from 203 to 135 million years ago.

**K-T boundary** The border between the Cretaceous and Tertiary periods.

**Mammals** Warm-blooded vertebrates that have hair and feed their young on milk.

**Marine** Found in the sea.

**Mesozoic era** The period of time, 250–65 million years ago, containing the Triassic, Jurassic and Cretaceous periods, when the dinosaurs lived.

**Meteorite** A meteor that lands on Earth.

**Microbe** A tiny organism, such as a bacterium.

**Molluscs** Invertebrates including snails, squids and octopuses.

**Omnivore** An animal that eats both animals and plants.

**Ornithischians** Dinosaurs that have hips similar to those of birds.

**Ornithomimids** Fast, long-legged dinosaurs resembling ostriches.

**Paleontologist** A scientist who studies fossils.

**Pangaea** The supercontinent formed at the end of the Permian period when all the continents of the Earth collided.

**Permian** The last period of the Palaeozoic era, lasting from 295 to 250 million years ago.

**Plankton** Microscopic organisms found in seas and lakes.

**Plesiosaurs** Marine reptiles living in the Mesozoic era.

**Podocarps** Types of conifer common in the Mesozoic era and still surviving today.

**Predator** An animal that hunts and kills animals for its food.

**Prey** An animal hunted or killed by another animal for food.

**Prosauropods** Early plant-eating dinosaurs living from the late Triassic period to the early Jurassic period.

**Pterosaurs** Flying reptiles that lived in the Mesozoic era.

**Reptiles** Cold-blooded, scaly vertebrates that usually lay eggs, such as crocodiles and snakes.

**Saurischians** Dinosaurs that have hips similar to those of lizards.

**Sauropods** Large, four-legged, plant-eating dinosaurs with enormous necks and tails.

**Scavenger** An animal that feeds on dead organisms.

**Stegosaurs** Plant-eating dinosaurs with bony plates or spines on their backs and tails.

**Synapsids** A group of early reptiles related to the mammals.

**Tethys Ocean** Separated the continent of Gondwana from the continent of Laurasia in the mid-Cretaceous period.

**Theropods** A group of saurischian dinosaurs that includes nearly all the carnivores.

**Triassic period** The first period of the Mesozoic era, lasting from 250 to 203 million years ago.

**Troodonts** Small Cretaceous hunting dinosaurs.

**Tsunami** A gigantic sea wave caused by a disturbance of the ocean floor, such as an earthquake.

**Vertebrae** The bones of the spine.

**Vertebrates** Animals with a backbone.

**Volcano** An opening in the Earth's crust which expels gases and lava.

**Warm-blooded** A warm-blooded animal uses its body chemistry to regulate its body temperature.

# The Extreme Hall of Fame

**Oldest known dinosaur:** *Eoraptor* ("Dawn Thief") is the oldest *named* dinosaur, about 228 million years ago.

**Smallest dinosaur:** *Microraptor* – 55 cm (22 in) long

**Smallest fossil skeleton:** *Mussaurus* – 18cm (7 in) long

**First egg discovered:** *Hypselosaurus* in 1869

**Largest egg discovered:** *Hypselosaurus* – 30 cm x 25 cm (11.8 x 9.8 in)

**Largest dinosaur:** *Brachiosaurus* – 25 m (82 ft) long and up to up to 80 tonnes

**Tallest dinosaur:** *Brachiosaurus* – 13 m (42.5 ft )

**Longest dinosaur:** *Diplodocus* – 28 m (92 ft)

**Biggest predator:** *Giganotosaurus* – 14 m (46 ft) and up to 8 tonnes

**Longest predator:** *Spinosaurus* – 18 m (59 ft)

# Credits

The publishers would like to thank the following sources for their kind permission to reproduce the pictures in this book.

Photograph indicators: *t* – top, *b* – bottom, *l* – left, *r* – right, *c* – centre

Pages are numbered as follows: Front endpaper 2–3; Meet the Dinosaurs 4–5; Old Timers 6–7; Micro Monsters 8–9; Super Heavyweights 10–11; Tough Guys 12–13; Sprinters and Plodders 14–15; Oddballs 16–17; Ferocious Beasts 18–19; The Longest and the Tallest 20–21; Masterminds 22–23; Big Heads 24–25; Extreme Eaters 26–27; Death and Extinction 28–29; Back endpaper 30–31